Lines of Sight

Also by Frances Presley:

The Sex of Art
Hula-Hoop
Linocut
Neither the One nor the Other, with Elizabeth James
Automatic Cross Stitch, with Irma Irsara
Somerset Letters
Paravane
Myne

Frances Presley

Lines of Sight

Shearsman Books
Exeter

Published in the United Kingdom in 2009 by
Shearsman Books Ltd
58 Velwell Road
Exeter EX4 4LD

ISBN 978-1-84861-039-2
First Edition

Acknowledgements

See page 114.

Contents

for Gavin
my neo-antiquarian and naked boy

Stone settings

Note on stone settings

Neolithic stone settings are arrangements of upright stones places in roughly geometric patterns or apparently randomly. They are unique to Exmoor, where they are by far the most common stone monument, and Hazel Eardley-Wilmot calls them 'Exmoor's special puzzle'.

Stones above Porlock

for Gavin and Keith

lent against
finger reach
kneeler
smallest in front   peeled stone

cuve out?
    curve out
carved down
caved

sheep shit
reeds   drawn reverse quavers
horizon
har   zone

explain vane
darblade
revels
splane   splice   rare
bare   breer   bre'er
brother

possibly slopes
ogham ruins all theories

space   down   hester
brown   each
sp/\ce   lark   bee

25 August 04

Hazel Eardley-Wilmot

The Author

acquainted with

                vagaries of language

does not

claim to be

more than

a serious amateur

                archaeologist

fifty years

the moor's

familiar

finding White Ladder

noticing   careful

thinking   unhurried

add to the

slender

                knowledge

Stone settings

per   pl ex

         moor

    two   three   or   four

    paral   lel   rows

    rec   tangles

    double   square

    squat   shape

almost regular   pattern   needs   another

stone   perceptible   just   under   turf

in drought a patch of starved grass will betray it

in wet weather   *feel it through soles*

Allow ! for

    s=o=t=v=o=e=n=r=e=s   grown

    shale   y

    de   composing

    re   moved

    Land   Rovered

           less

incom   prehen

plete   sible

                                                        OUTLIER

guess the riddle

no analogy

slight

resemblance to Scottish *four-posters*

            lack a centre

                            a dominant position within the frame

some patterns are completely enigmatic

Stone settings x 3

'fate derives from fando, that is from speaking'

for Barbara x 2

three   rows   of
three   evenly   spaced
well   aligned

three   and   thrice

                 Thre   Werd

Systrys

hand   in   hand

                               chanting

      thrice to thine, and thrice to mine
      peace the charm

god   desses   of

destinie   his   terrific

daughters   wretched   old

     women   arm   in

     arm   ba   bar

     bar(e

          i   an

White ladder

entirely   chance

cold   spring

short   grass

double   row

quartz   stones

sandstone   slabs

one   stride

two

between

ladder   like

slow   search

not   wall

not   bank

not   boundary

shining   stone

ploughed   out

road				metalling
one		by		one
deceptively				swallowed
boggy				source
		Kinsford		
		Cunet		(io)
Girl	=	Kunti	=	Spring

Brer

On Exmoor as well as triangles there are rectangles and parallelograms and rhomboids like a series of Euclidean exercises. He said that it can't be Euclidean geometry except by accident and without understanding the angles. Even the Egyptians . . . . and this was so much later and so much less. As for the rhomboid, he can only remember the rhombus, which is a sort of lop-sided square. If it was a rhomboid it would have to be three dimensional and one of the stones would be suspended in the sky. A rhombus is a flat fish. Only those without memories roam the moor at night. An oblique equilateral parallelogram. How can we follow these parallel lives? Lost stag hounds mud red and howling, facing opposite directions. A quadrilateral of which only opposite sides and angles are equal. Quad bike pass by. She is worried that he has no over trousers, but he cannot be threatened by rain or cold. Sphagnum, she says, under our boots, and they seem more precarious and waterlogged. The stones at the circle look smaller than in memory or in the photographs, and are known as miniliths. Lichen micro crusts substitute for decoration, and there is nothing grey in their green. We turn to face the camera hidden in her jacket turning into the wind and rain. *From here to Withypool circle is a precisely straight line of six and a half miles.* But they would not have had lines of sight, he says. They could not have known, and there will always be a straight line between two points.

bre-er
out of the briar patch
sweet brier
out of the bare earth
he came
brer

an edge
e
merge
an angle

Withypool circle

It's time to move forward and not back in spite of this handwriting. Reconstruct each particle con(densed) trail in a game of connect-the-dots. She can't hear the bagpipes, only the drums rehearsing for st george's day. He is talking about the triumfeminate, and the least remembered, Ann, who is Lepidus, the most passionate and daring of the three. We are back at Howarth, and I'm not sure if we ever left. Here it is, the white out, the zero visibility. Mist and bird song. Listen to the lark, I heard it on the video. Nothing has the same continuity, the same lack of pauses. I am familiar with the map, but there are no marked paths. It can be approached from both sides of the hill, from the road to Withypool Cross, or from Worth Lane. I am suffering from late-onset nominative determinism, and all the paths have my initials. In Celia Haddon's website you walk up to the tumulus, line up Tudball Splats on the opposite slope and walk towards these. *If the heather had been high I might not have found it at all.* Today nothing is lined by sight. Dark circles must be gorse. You have to imagine them, I encourage her. She is more interested in the ponies, and one with a foal we can barely see. It looks dead to me. No, I think it's just sleeping, I saw its head lift. Yes, they're tough, aren't they, not like sheep. There is no market for them. She tells me to go ahead and see if there is any sign of a path leading off the path which might lead to the stones but there isn't. A moment's sound of *may may may*, before rejoining.

Dina Portway Dobson

Preface to *The Archaeology of Somerset*

Everything cannot be – included –

Attempt to summarize

to the end of 1930

To theorize significance

is another

difficult matter

Today the archaeologist needs   attributes of the bird

      or the mole

                    the help of an aeroplane

      or a spade

Marshalling   patient

for the worker of the future

          'Out of monuments, names, words, proverbs, traditions,
          private records and evidences, fragments of stories,
          passages of books that concern not story

industrious persons

we

do save and recover

from the deluge of time'   *Francis Bacon*

That flood sweeps along now

faster than ever before

Record

more than ever

what is left

and so to

place it

high and dry

out of reach

                 of the waters

plotted on

¼ inch to a mile Ordnance Survey

not possible to secure accuracy

working to this scale

each find to its own parish

vestiges

left

to

                                                us

Porlock circle

blown over with the ripple
declension of fractals
finding its lake in the dipping stone

this natural geological
recumbation travelator

wind heave lifts paper
lifts plates throws rain
scatter across the page

concrete poetry
scatters
across the page
in ....
and that may be the problem

what did I mean?
her name too clair
so is mine too frank

hold pad down with difficulty
follow sheep into the hollow
or crater
of bog reed bottom

one stone over that was up before

continuity of thought is blown sideways
with the reeds
in spite of all that modern
clothing allows

damp page
all this will disappear in dots

23 May 05

7 x 7

major arteries running out of London

>   *resolve*
>   *uphold*
>   *extremists*

everyone's in pitch

>   the same in . . . ?
>   the same *as* in . . . ?
>   the same
>   in
>   Spain

the report on track
the wheels
feel them beneath your soles

>   the changes are as follows
>   no westbound service

>   sorry about that
>   I made a mistake there
>   no eastbound service

From the air

Air-photographs for archaeological rather than military purposes were taken by the Denkmalschutzkommando. *One cannot but admire the scientific enthusiasm of a country which could remember archaeology in the midst of a world war.*

think

       mark

             shoot

Withypool tracks

1

he adds a dimension.

an edge

        why are you so

                                edgy?

        downward curve of the

                        Some defs of dys explored
                     Some current theories of dys
                         Signs & symptoms of dys

        can I change my mind
    after all
westwater is there on the map

2

You can walk along here and you get to this track.
They're trying to get some shade as well.
The pathfinder series no longer exists 1:25000.
What I suggest we do is we walk up to this crossing point to give us
some idea of the distance involved, then we can hack – bash – our way
up to there. If we walk as far as . . . . Where the hedge curls off . . . .
At some point . . . .
We meet the other track . . . .
. . . the other track.
Surveyed in the seventies, published in the eighties. You can print
down to this scale and smaller.
It goes from one track to the next and I don't know why. This tough
grass I only know in Welsh, gwamaan, mountain grass, but I don't

know it in English. And the mane of this one looks like . . .

This is definitely the tumulus.

We've done one thing right, haven't we?

This is all going to look so flat. Did I take that? I can take another one. You can always delete it.

Half way between . . . .

Just slightly to the right is . . .

Isn't that the path we've just come up?

We came across that way.

I don't think we were really on a path.

Quincuncial

after Sir Thomas Browne

Arbores ordines Quincuncem orders five   *the garden*

pari et directa so Trees

intervallo omnia the handsomely so

sitas perpulchre rows disposed set

rectos in and or together

that through every not number

a prospect side only of

regular was owing unto Trees

angularity left this the but

and on name Quintuple the

                   the charm   Rurall strangling order Tile one

                                 charm strangling this a four

                 against weeds order chalked corners

                        Dodder was while Tile and

                      Tetter contrived they at one

                         in which was a magick

                the which intention contrivance to

                    middle though was and diffuse

                 of ridiculous rational good magick

              their ridiculous was contrivance way

Out made Battle or Battles   *the war*

of two the the each

this remarkable Cuneus sheare made

figure forms and and of

were of Forceps wedge half

a to a environ thereof

Rhombus break body and composed

the or the defeat out

wedge work forceps the of

invented into to power Souldiery

        the game   The disposed they being eighth

                      Proci of played themselves they

                          or their at an set

      Prodigall men Penelope hundred fifty

          Paramours when for and four

                stones one they that the

                  on in called hit game

            either the Penelope was game

          hit Penelope middle and stones

        game was which which one

Culbone

_____ feel of detachment

within this catchment

dentate covers foil mayhem
their hemming and humming
so much closer
make still
remuse the heart?

kil beun

they have chosen the porch
        to play games
I did not understand the reference to dominoes
or the clue for top point

        point
low
        dir
na

do the clocks change?

                    she asked   in The Ship at Porlock

                        she had not seen him for weeks
                        he was on exercises
                        and now she has a cold
                        and wants flannelette

where pen_ goes/go

                        dissent
is allowed

make this where
make this collar turn against
                        cooler tune
hunched

to speak one word against
is so negative
                        you are being so negative

        one word
        a single word

                        nonsense

commsate?

in break
fingers on the rood?
touching breaking   cr mmml
spalce splane
ripping of wood ? word

                on a white bowl
clear glass
                white walls

coldrement?
                enlightenment
                    no regrets no memories
white candles

Charlotte

                Charlotte   1958

                      Bell died

imperilled
           impanelled
with two small teddies

I remember the trademark argument
red typed
           tipped

                  butterfly on holly

a crack in the panel
      }{   in the uni   verse

sunflower had

            head down

they cd not have their fun
a misprint for sun
for three months
they cd not have their Sun

I will not go to yearnor

Non sense
~~leaking~~ me and tpane
up through the winds is all gone

taken without flash
waiting for the flash to leave

one word is too much

for smooth words

I could have said more
one word is enough

I didn't know it would be open

1 October 05

Culbone, or Kil Beun (church of Beuno), is hidden in woods on the coastal footpath, beyond Porlock Weir, and there is no direct sunlight during the winter months: I was writing in the half-light, allowing language to form and reform. It was the day after the New Labour party conference when Walter Wolfgang was ejected for saying the word 'nonsense'.

Arranged triangle

Evening? I suppose it is
these blackberries
  grabbed a few on the way

through tree comes
wind and light
no flat horizon

in dark wood
no bright hunt
or perfect spurs
court dress
                      drew uccello

he sang for saint george
last night
our accordionist

and on her breast she wore
the red red rose
of england

        cold deeds valnit

trowelling the pencil
turning over the page

choked pine
caution
                    CAUTION

bracken rising
to the apex of my triangle
yellow diminish

is it evening?
felled conifer

long triangular shadow blows to hinkley point

Arranged quincunx

morning
sunless
stop on new
unfolding seat

thought for the day was thanatos
terrorism is not as simple as

Jonathan Sacks
you can't blame it all
on the death wish

I was waking in the night
worrying over C
falling
in the garden
her song about falling:

     being careful
     so careful
     I was being
       so
     I was being

       so
     without warning
     it goes
     my leg
     and I was falling

     on the freshly turned
     earth
     on my back
     no purchase
     the dark earth

shouting
but no one hears
(radio on)
for twenty minutes
crawling back

the clue was:
  used to
  formerly
  some
  time

I would be your legs
         your arms
dark day
new year
it is not the only cause

                                Hopcott
                        2–3 October 05

Culbone stone

cross made   out
                 of the circle

incised   i

                                      taken by the stone
                                      worked through

ribs
implode

implant
chosen lines

26 November 05

No rider could penetrate the pine angles
                warfed and wisted
few walkers would

        a wheeled cross of the Dark Ages
                askew
on its upright stone

the cross is neither
upright
                        nor diagonal
neither St George
           nor St Andrew

its top quadrant is ten minutes to one
                    and the stem
         equal in length to the diameter
                    projects from four o'clock

this is not clumsiness
              clumsiness
the circle and straight lines are the work of a good craftsman

then why?
      it seems   at best   disrespectful

the line of the stone enough for local people
         who knew it was far down
                    the steep slope
                      to the sea
    the slant of the stem
           to help
             strangers

A broken rear red light, the gate warning. She would stand at the gate and get paid to open it. Why are these trees so bent? She is losing her short term memory. Why does the cross point in that direction? She thinks it was pointing to kilbeun, church of Beuno. The stone was found flat on its face in 1940. Who found it? I want to name the gamekeeper. He has lost his short term memory, but is drawn on by elements of architectural interest. Later we found him walking towards the 'Far Pavilions' of the holiday camp. Is it possible to propitiate the trees? He tells us she was convinced that the Chinese had discovered America, when the only genuine thing about the map is the paper: it's based on the Mercator system, which they would not have had and above all, on this map, China is not the centre of the universe. We cannot go beyond the stone to search for the stone row as it's private and fenced off. I dreamt I was walking through the town at night but the street was full of red kapok or candyfloss. I had to tear through it, stile slippery in the rain. It is wrong to talk about intelligence as a substance as if it were a substance. We can talk about inference. Why are those buildings empty, why are those woods empty? Who has scattered these lumps of carrot. That is not a gun emplacement but a covert. Is it a covert or a cover? These simple flowers, periwinkle. *I can't make sentences in my head now. I can speak and listen, but I can't write.*

Two oaks and a triangle

thicker girth
not biodegradable
no need for secateurs

stay here
less than three
headland

ten years
taken out
stemming primate

It's funny that the leaves haven't fallen off

ever bronze
clinging acorns
fruit   fruit   fruit

new stems
new growth
these leaf formations

      .   .
      .

here the rings end
no further
to reason

expert cut
clear incision
—

                                          new sidestem
                                          is it too thin
                                       will it continue?

                                          how to prune
                                          what remains
                                                 -

                                       can a replacement
                                       be a re placement?
                                    too much competition

                                          to rise above
                                       or simply to leave
                                          and let her go

                            .   .

                                 .

arranged stone
triangle
her boots

any self respecting deer could have its feet in

the stone that is only a stone
at the base of brambles
between two beech trees

anxiety for the oak
which must either thrive
or

nettled frenzy
these laurels we do not want
though less invasive

mind shift
gear change
text expected
cyclist

at the oaks planted in memory of my mother, Selworthy woods
17 Feb 07

Whiteladder revisited

           on   a
           dia   gon
           al   you
           will   not
           stay   on
           the

white   grass
memories   of   snow

      and   what did i know?

you are   throwing
                          a fallen fence
                             wire and posts

                             back to the boundary

i need the beginning

           cow   pat
           re   lated
           slate   crop
           ed   out
           quartz

      we   the

                                      ladder

                 l   _

                 _   d

                 l   ae   d

22 October 07

44

Longstones

Triscombe stone

Which wood are we in? Maritime sessile oak. No, which wood are we in? I thought it was scrub oak. Triscombe stone half fixed in concrete, a hazard to cars at the meeting point, in a declining sun. It is thought to be from the Bronze Age. The ancient of days lowers himself onto its cold stone which provides a convenient seat. Travellers are not explorers and there would be no need for elaborate sighting. We read about the recent wet ground conditions that have caused roadside damage by Dead Woman's Ditch. Vehicles spill out onto the heath. She says that she is interested in rock art and that there is a pattern to it. She has been driven to many aboriginal sites. *There is proof of global warming at last.* In 1991 when I was forced to scan five newspapers and discovered for the first time that we only had eighty years left, the pink columns of the FT provided the most accurate and factual information, and were most likely to provide source references. She says that only two degrees of warmth makes such a difference, and that was true in the Bronze Age. Above all I want to try and avoid rotating the image. I want it to be properly aligned from the first moment that I preview the scan. I can then clean the document, decrease the colour depth and optimise the image, unless there is significant artwork. On Exmoor the rocks are artless, they are earme, impoverished. The long highways, who travelled and why are you walking below me through watery lane?

Triscombe stone   (4)

Smaller than I remember, not even shoulder-high. People were
shorter in Coleridge's bed, and we were closer together, not knowing
how, moving towards and turning away, in and out of sleep. Why
are you balancing on one leg on top of the stone, arms outstretched,
taller than I remember? You say that I started it. Please note that
this should not be set in concrete. She wants to know who died
recently. I died recently, he says, balancing on ski sticks. He is too
old for the hare path, which was never used by hares. I thought she
said the 'herr' path, but it wasn't the men's path exactly; it was the
'heer' path, the group path, the army path, the hurrying unheavenly
host. She wants us to take 'the middle way', but the modern road
has deviated, as the ancient beech hedge shows. She tries to sit him
down. I can't sit there, he protests, it's a thorn bush. I could make
you a crown. Peat and small loose stones. We are listening to larks,
a small bird flying through the sea mist which he can't see, and he
is hearing another even more continuous noise, which we say is a
plane though he doesn't believe us, until we see a small biplane, or
perhaps a 'mav', micro aerial vehicle. They want to remove the trig
point which is on a cairn, as trig points are no longer required. She
calls it a concrete stump. Everyone can be found in any place at all,
located by satellite and GPS, global positioning system, which could
be used for peaceful as well as military purposes. George W Bush
in a new directive reflects renewed US government commitment
to maintaining GPS as a global leader in satellite navigation. I was
deceived about the direction, he says, – I thought it was the opposite
way. No one needs the trig point to find the way, but the longstone
would be a necessary sign.

Operation Mountain Thrust

opposition opposition
opposition writ

crack consensus
acceded Reid

southern NATO
forward bases
short troops

pathfinder Unit
battlefield relative

Para complex
swoop screens
scurrying seven

frenzied forget
resemblance same

cock- although
video match

aggression ties
helicopters fuse

energised crack
writ South

Memorial

lay this here
as a tribute
to whoever
is left

he is not here
to protect
to defend
to stand up

ways are waves
taken from tossed grass
minute heads
make moment
not mine

I am in her lens
this takes me mo

              wo

                   over ?

and travels
the length of my spinal nerve

who is not here
who is not with us
as must be
as is

At a WW2 memorial, near Brendon Two Gates, 10 July 06

Triscombe stone (2)

I was dreading this journey. Coleridge's bedroom looks barer and some books are already in boxes. We walked to Triscombe stone along the ridge from Dead Woman's Ditch in bright October light. On the hills there is a strong wind blowing, and in spite of the warm (too warm) sun the leaves are moving. I can't begin to treat these beech leaves as word counters in a philosophical argument, because that would create a lattice work of confined reinforcement. Walking, not digressing, (the brackets help), the edge of the overgrown beech hedge and its unstill leaves and twigs, avoiding the bridle path, as the sheep, gathering oddly in a white semicircle to the side of the path, had avoided the young horse riders, before we understood why (no more human coincidences). This is not the outskirts, hem or fringe of a habitation and I will not be travelling back into the city. This hedge is not even a threshold or a liminal zone, but its own border, as a life should be. The stone is there, neglected as ever, and greener than memory as she turns her lens, this time, to the white fungi.

Hare

how do hare tare along?

alkitotle
antle-beer
blogging
buckle to
chun
quean
coltee
cuff
daps
haggage
hobby
lanching
lipped
lewstery
paddle
palch
pistering   and   whistering
pigsnye
querking
rabble-rote
rag   row   tering
rex-bush
rigmutton
rumpstall
ripping
rixy
roil
roundshaving
rouzeabout
rubbacrock
sprey
sproil
steehopping

stertling
stroil
swapping
tare
thirl
tourn
vittee
zidle-mouth
zwir thy tourn

VOCABULARY for

explaining uncouth Expressions, and interpreting barbarous
Words and Phrases.

Hare	her; by the Exmoorians also used for *she*
Alkitotle	a silly elf or foolish oaf (Perhaps a foolish creature, troubled with fits and epilepsies to which the Elk (in Latin, Alce) is said to be subject. Q)
Antle-beer	cross-wise, irregular
Blogging	looking sullen
Buckle to	gird up the loins
Chun or Quean	woman. Q? – But a quean formerly meant a whore, and generally now denotes a bad sort of woman.
Coltee	to act the hobby-horse, to be as playful as a young colt
Cuff	to exchange stories, as if contending for the mastery; or to canvas a story between one and another. Vid. Homer IL. Lib. 1.
Daps	the aptes, aptitudes or attitudes: the exact likeness of another, in all his gestures and motions.
Haggage	hag ridden or slattern
Hobby	to play the hobby-horse, to be at romps with men
Lanching	*quasi* launching, or making long strides
Lipped	to be let pass; to be loose and free; and sometimes the breaking out of the stitches in needlework
Lewstery	to bustle and stir about like a lusty wench
Paddle	signifies not only to dabble in the water, but also to make too free with liquor, or to drink freely
Palch	to stalk or walk on softly
Pistering and whistering	Telling stories to the disadvantage of others in whispers.
Pigsnye	a fairy (ab Islandic. *puke*, daemon)
Querking	the deep, slow breathing of a person in pain
Rabble-rote	a repetition of a long story
Ragrowtering	(*quasi* rag-rough-tearing) playing at romps, and thereby rumpling, roughening and tearing the clothes to rags

Rex-bush	or rather rix (ab. Angl.Sax. *rixan*), a rush; a bush of tuft of rushes
Rigmutton-rumpstall	may sometimes mean a rammish ridgel; but is generally used to denote a wanton wench that is ready to ride upon men's backs
Ripping	taking off the rind and exposing our nakedness; or ripping up our characters and laying open all our faults
Rixy	quarrelsome, scolding
Roil	a big, ungainly slammakin; a great awkward blowze or hoyden
Roundshaving	spoke-shaving, reprimanding roundly
Rouzeabout	a restless creature, never easy at home, but roaming from place to place. Also a sort of large pease, which from their regular globosity will hop or roll about more than others.
Rubbacrock	a filthy slattern, that is as black as if she were continually rubbing herself against a boiler or a kettle.
Sprey	sprack, spruce and clever
Sproil	a capacity of motion, ability to *sprawl* about, and be active
Steehopping	gadding about idly to hear and carry news (Possibly from the British *Ystiferion* eve-droppings, and so may denote the conduct of eve-droppers, who hearken for news under windows; but more probably from the Saxon *staer historia*, and *hoppan gestire*, and so is expressive of the talebearer's chief employment, viz to carry stories from house to house.
Stertling roil	a wag-tail Blowze, or one whose motion is directed like a ship by the rudder in her stern.
Stroil	(from *struggle*) Strength and agility
Swapping	big, large, unwieldy
Tare	to bustle through business, to be stirring and active. "How do hare tare along", ie how doth she go on, or make her way in the world? How doth her diligence and assiduity succeed?

Thirl	gaunt and lank, thin and lean
Tourn	a spinning wheel; so called from its turning round
Vittee	to go well, fitly and successfully
Zidle-mouth	the mouth awry, or more extended on one side than the other
Zwir thy tourn	Quhir, or whirl round thy spinning wheel with speed; let thy diligence be proclaimed by its zwirring, or quhirring noise

Strawberries

strawberriesstrawberriesstrawberriesstrawberriesstrawberriesstrawberries
strawberriesstrawberriesstrawberriesstrawberriesstrawberriesstrawberries
strawberriesstrawberriesstrawberriesstrawberriesstrawberriesstrawberries
strawberriesstrawberriesstrawberriesstrawberriesstrawberriesstrawberries
strawberriesstrawberriesstrawberriesstrawberriesstrawberriesstrawberries
strawberriesstrawberriesstrawberriesstrawberriesstrawberriesstrawberries
strawberriesstrawberriesstrawberriesstrawberriesstrawberriesstrawberries
strawberriesstrawberriesstrawstrawstrawstrawstrawstrawstrawstrawstraw
strawstrawstrawstrawstrawstrawstrawstrawstrawstrawstrawstrawstraw
strawstrawstrawstrawstrawstrawstrawstrawstrawstrawstrawstrawstraw
strawstrawstrawstrawstrawstrawstrawstrawstrawstrawstrawstrawstraw
rawrawrawrawrawrawrawrawrawrawrawrawrawrawrawrawrawraw
rawrawraw rawrawrawrawrawrawrawrawraw

strawberries
straw   berries
straw
raw

"that's why they call us strawberries, 'cause we get the rocks and we
will have oral sex"

Naked boy drunk

he is a big quartz boulder
astride the line of parish boundaries

its spine directs the eye
south east
marking the head
of the Tone

before the water-table dropped

did they worship the stone *as* the stream?

water worship persisted
worried St Augustine

> the stone *as* the stream >

long after he
was said to be drunk

petrified
for his sinister

> as the stream

who must go down
to drink
at midnight
from the source

Naked boys beaten

he was a boy
stripped naked made to
stand on the stone
walk around and shiver

from a ritual of beating
the bounds of the
Royal Forest of Exmoor
learning the mark-stones

on the wild borders
beaten by boundary riders
impressing the limits
reminders sharp physical rough

named four naked boys
by 1822 map markers
four parishes which touch
each supplied a victim

after Jack Hurley

....

her foot note

obvious white boulder
separates ordinary parishes
false analogy no
local evidence supports his
                    fantasy

The naked boy David

which milliband can we see
which miliband do you prefer

naked in formation
greenwashed

Naked Boy as linguistic confusion

Cnoc
meaning hillock
in Celtic
or *knock*
in Old English

Bu
or
boy
has a stately pedigree
meaning ox or bull or cow
shared by the earliest farmers
before the tribes parted

one of Homer's epithets for Hera
Queen of Heaven
was 'ox-eyed'
bo-opis

if Knackyboy meant
hill of cattle
did Saxons anglicise it as
Naked Boy?

cattle from the Common
took all the prizes at local shows
a bloom on their coats

and the Irish saga
Tain Bo Cuailnge
celebrates
the Cattle-Raid of Cooley
launched by Queen Maeve of Connaught
against Cuchulain of Ulster to steal
if she could
the dun bull of his herd

Naked boy

1

nest more
perforce
range up

naked boy
nay   nay   ced
head truculent cede

it has its spine
like a boy leaning
like a boy stripped bare

a green coat for the quartz
a pelt
let us pelt

2

the naked boy
rests into the stone
put him up against

what did he say

he's disappearing
he's going to turn right
he's climbing over the gate

two bodies that prop each other up
one animal one human

3

fossilised face
worn down
ossified
turn away

we have gone down
we have gathered
we have emerged

watching the wind farm

leave
drink
protest

high flown pheasant

4

he holds a lap
it shapes a lap

SHIPS THAT WE NEED?

SHAPES

shiplap
just the common name for over
lapping
slates   and plates

we have overlapped

12 April 07

Caratacus stone

'failure is not an option'
GWB

leans sideways	C
at an awkward angle	A
this is not the way to strain	R
gradual ceding	Ā
call it quits	A
double or quits	C
my double trouble	I
character gouged	
smooth mouthed	
leaning tower	
kept leaning	
lean times	
monitored always	
identify me with	
for nepus	И
chipped off	E
the block	P
pasted back	U
with pale pink gum	S

24 June 07

Note on the inscription

'The stone is so remote from railways, and the ways of Latinists, that it has hardly ever been seen by an epigraphist'

It is impossible to clearly show the inscription by means of an untouched photograph. So that the sizes and shapes of the letters, and the spacing of the inscription, can be readily seen, they have been outlined at the expense of naturalness

CARĀACI or Caratacus – Welsh national hero of early Roman days, betrayed by Queen Catismandu and taken in chains to Rome
NEPUS = Nepos (Romano-British reading) Sister's son, descendent, kinsman, son, grandson, nephew

One of the pieces was distinctly inscribed with Ͷ and exactly fitted the fracture immediately preceding the EPVS. The N was cut reversed – a not uncommon error even nowadays

It is to a local hillman, unversed in archaeology, we must turn for the key to the re-discovery of the missing Ͷ, for its jealous protection during many months, and for its fixing to the inscription in the exact position and with commendable skill

Carat – represents the passive participle of the verb, which is in Welsh car-u, to love

West Anstey longstone

here   ti (l)   la
my deepest breath
startling deer

stertling roil
on the ridge

she's here at last
the 'veiled lady'

shepherde of the stream
no strange or rambling

look after each other
each
all one

with a plantering bosom
my own things get done last

patched   patchouli
absterrent   hardering

made hepworth
veiled but more expressive
than a gormley

look there's a small orange

the anatomy of sandstone
will not pister

'd'où viens-tu bergère'?
not from the tour eiffel
or the mobile mast

tired of that ancient world
her masts are flowing   familial
her masts

24 June 07

Buttery stone

for Patrick, who is leaving Brisbane
where there is no more water

where are you
                at the stone

ferned   hearned
plithered
shivered out for the boundary

just say hi again

you're underneath that big beech

dsn't seem to protrude

definity source
          a pond
after so much rain

beech   tree
hedge

not against wind
we have won wind

the house is standing against
abutting the hillside
                    abetting

buttery butts
the water but
cannot save austral ia

          this sliver of stone

compressed
glivers
revested

14 August 07

Notes

Some of the poems in 'Stone settings' and 'Longstones' form part of a collaboration and multi-media performance with the poet Tilla Brading, who was also the Assistant Custodian of Coleridge Cottage until 2006. I am grateful to Robert Wilson-North, the Exmoor archaeologist, and Hazel Riley, archaeologist at English Heritage, who met us for field visits and book room discussions. Their book *The Field Archaeology of Exmoor*, English Heritage, 2001, has been an important resource. Hugh and Rachel Thomas have given us generous access to Hazel Eardley-Wilmot's archive.

I have made extensive use of Hazel Eardley-Wilmot's *Ancient Exmoor* (The Exmoor Press, 1983), and especially the sections on stone settings, the stone row White Ladder, and Culbone Stone.

p.10   The epigraph by Isidore of Seville is quoted by Marina Warner in *From the beast to the blonde*, Vintage, 1994

p.13   Aubrey Burl *From Carnac to Callanish*, Yale, 1993

p.15   Dina Portway Dobson *The Archaeology of Somerset*, Methuen, 1931. The italicised quotation is Francis Bacon *The Advancement of Learning*, Second Book, 1605, reprinted Benton, 1952

p.19   Alexander Keiller & O G S Crawford *Wessex from the air*, Clarendon, 1928

pp.21–22 Thomas Browne *The Garden of Cyrus; or, the Quincunciall, Lozenge, or Network plantations of the Ancients, artificially, naturally, mystically considered*, 1658 repr. Dent, 1906

pp.41–43 *An Exmoor scolding in the propriety and decency of Exmoor language, between two sisters, Wilmot Moreman and Thomasin Moreman, as they were spinning*, Penny & Son, 1771

p.44   *Rethinking prostitution: purchasing sex in the 1990s*, ed. G & A Scamble, Routledge, 1997

p.46   Jack Hurley *Legends of Exmoor*, The Exmoor Press, 1973

p.47   Hazel Eardley-Wilmot 'The Naked Boy – a reappraisal' *Exmoor Review*, 38, pp 41-42

p.52   Alfred Vowles *The History of the Caratacus stone*, 1939

Female figures

Onde

And when I was thirty yers old and halfe
God sent me a bodily sekeness
in which I lay iii dayes and iii nights

And on the iii night I wened oftentimes
to have passyd and so wened
they that were with me

And in youngith yet   I thought great
sweeme to die but for nothing
was in earth that me lekid to leven for

I durid till day and be than my body
was dede fro the middis
downewards as to my feleing

Then was I stered to be sett upright
for to have more fredam
of my herte to be at God's will

My eyen were sett uprightward into hevyn
But I assented to sett them
in the face of the crucifix if I might

After this my sight began to failen and it was
all derke about me in the chamber
as it had be night

After this the other party of my body began
to dyen so ferforth that I had ony feleing
with shortness of onde

Julian's view

'he shewed a littil thing, the quantitye of an hesil nutt in the palme of my
hand; and it was as round as a balle.'

BEWARE CONSTRUCTION TRAFFIC

I always wanted a tennis ball
I've got one at home

Project: The Hostry
Completion Date: Spring 2009

Where did you find that dirty old thing?

Morgan Ashurst welcomes you to the <u>Hostry</u> project.
Whatever your reason for being here, we aim to make your visit as
safe and enjoyable as possible

Stay there. There's a car coming.
X507 JAH

It is important that everyone has an induction before entering any
work area. Please follow any instructions given to you by Morgan
Ashurst personnel.

Let's all play a game with it and pass it to each other.

If you see anything that might affect your safety or the safety of others

Come over here, please
It's mine

FAMILIES GIVEN A GLIMMER OF HOPE

Mummy
Stop shouting. Don't shout
Give me that ball, please

Norwich Cathedral
11 August 08

Inclosyd

as the herte in the bouke

halseth us

the flesh in the skyne

beclosyth

us

the bonys in the flesh

as the body is clad in cloth

so arn we   cladde

love wrappith us

Anne R

she wore Elizabeth's robes   and her motto

        semper eadem

always the same   always   the same

same   stress

        small state craft

sempre   forte

    the safety of small rooms

          simperering susans

sempstress   and starcher

           nearest to my person

    Margaret Tyzack as Anne   in black and white pre-MT
      V bagged eyes   lines descending on sleepless
      O, reasonable Augusta!   considering nights
       O, lucid expostulator   in double chin
     advancing while   godolphins dance backwards
    pearls strung on stout neck   the global shell infolds

dost sometimes counsel take   and sometimes tea

    brilliant light shone down upon the stately Queen Anne service
       shone through the thinness of the shallow flowered cups
    tea, cried Miriam, should never be drunk from cold white cups

sip down to the pattern   sit down to action

Speaking by letters

"It must, said Maynwaring afterwards, have been like
addressing a statue filled with earth."

My dear Mrs Freeman if ever you should forsake me, I would have
nothing more to do with the world, but make another abdycation, for
what is a Crown when ye support of it is gon
your poor unfortunat faithfull Morly

Morley who is still so lame that she can hardly walk the length of the
room, and that with two sticks

     a creeple   inclined so much to vaypours

My poor heart is so tender I durst not tell you what was the matter
with me, because I know if I had begun to speak, I should not have
been fit to be seen by anybody . . . I fancied . . . that you have a wrong
and hard thought of me. I should be very glad to know what they are
that I might clear myself, but let it be in writing
for I dare not venture to speak with you

The difficulties I labour under at this time are so great and so uneasy
to me, that they will not suffer me any longer to keep my thoughts to
myself, and I choose this way of explaining them to you,
rather than endeavour to speak
and not be able to go on . . .

whether they are call'd Whigs or Torys, not to be tyed to one, nor
to ye other, for if I should be soe unfortunate as to fall into ye hands
of ether, I shall look upon my self tho I have the name of Queen, to
be in realety but their slave

Whoever of ye Whigs thinks I am to be Hecktor'd or frighted into a
Complyance tho I am a woman, are mightily mistaken in me

They have been disputing my authority, and are certainly designing
. . . to tear that little prerogative the Crown has to peaces . . . how is
it possible . . . ever to take these people into my bosom?

I have this business of the Peace so much at heart

I can't yet walk, but I hope by the time that public business
requires my being in town
I shall get strength enough to bear the jolting of a coach

from **Windsor Forest**

after Pope

Her cereal gifts   here serial slips

in waving prospect   wave to prospect

And nodding tempt   and noddies tempt

the reaper's hand   to the ten pence band

Rich industry smiling   ~~shits~~ on the plains

Peace and plenty tell   a Gordon reigns

When Anthony sends   her eager sons to war

Some thoughtless town with ease and plenty blest

Near and more near   close the lines   invest

Sudden they seize the amazed defenceless maize

And high in air   Murkana's standard flies

See!   pheasant   springs   wings

            plumes   unfold   gold

                  wound   blood   ground

dyes   scarlet eyes

And high in air   the standard harrier dies

Anne's view

In her foreground is the recently re-paved Wellington square, and a smart poster board for the Regal Theatre: 'Donated by Minehead Town Council on behalf of the people of Minehead'. An almost young couple and a red Routemaster advertise a new production of SUMMER HOLIDAY. The board stands in front of a bright municipal begonia bed, and a large spreading lime tree: the one allowable tree. Beyond is what used to be the old road to Porlock, which is now by-passed.

On the other side of the road an elderly man in a blue v-neck jumper emerges with a newspaper folded in his hand. Anne would have seen the *Plume of Feathers* coaching inn, which survived the fire of 1791, but it was demolished in the 1960s, and now she is looking at a white retail box.

LINENS   brand names at discount prices
Bedding
Curtains
Nets
Towels
& so much more

Ocean Catch

New manager. Fresh fish.
'Today fishing. Get your bait here.'

BUTTERFLIES   foliage   CAFE

We're all different, thank goodness. I only wish I had your memory. If only I could remember names. I could go to a meeting of top civil servants and within two minutes I'd forgotten who I was talking to. And that was because I wasn't really interested. For instance, here's a list of the church coffee morning. I only remember the woman who sits on my left and talks about pink rabbits occasionally. Bartley? Backley. I can't go this week. Flu jab on the 30th. Arthritis hanging around. Down to 3 milligrams. Do you take co-codamol? And the BBC breakfast programme is absolute codswallop. Biggest issue is the European Union and this treaty and the BBC don't tell us <u>anything</u> about it. News in brief, that's all you get.

BUTTER   the canopy   FLIES

Note on Queen Anne's statue

'An uncommonly fine piece with great skill in the rendering of the details of the clothes . . . The statue is made of alabaster and attributed to Francis Bird. It would not do discredit to him.'

South and West Somerset Pevsner, Penguin, 1958

'. . . a statue of Queen Anne, presented by a Swede who became Sir J. Bancks, and in 1696 married a rich widow of the Luttrells (this statue – formerly in the church, now in Wellington Square – was carved by Francis Bird, a protégé of Grinling Gibbons)

What you will not find is an industry which supplied the stone for Queen Anne's statue, though the industry was thriving when Thomas Gerard mentioned it in his 'Particular Description of the County of Somerset' (1633): 'Att this place in our tyme a Dutch man hath found out mynes of excellent Alabaster, which they much use for Tombes and Chimney pieces. . . . for variety of mixtures and colours . . .

Portrait of Exmoor JBH Peel   Robert Hale, 1970

Also inscribed on the canopy:

Captvre of Gibraltar	1704	Vnion with Scotland	1707
Battle of Blenheim	1704	Ovdenarde	1708
		Malplaquet	1709
Battle of Ramillies	1706	Treaty of Vtrecht	1713

Thatcher at the Guildhall

your pupils are hollow
(o)

between the eyebrows
contraction
w

marble nose job
lost in a nostril

an ear hole
tucked under the coiff.
ure

muffled by the perm
anent wave

down drawn lines
frame the lip

neck wrinkles
sign a cut

the severity

I think I am being watched

she is safe behind glass
I am reflected
head height to her waist

– Bizarre innit?

men in white shirts
black tie and trousers

– Hello
I'm number 6
– You're not a number,
you're a free man

she is poised

– ready to dash –

brow beat

against the case

her jacket is ruled in lines
buttoned up

three   large
large
but   tons

what is held back
what cannot be given

book curling
in hand

the law in my grasp

our Stationery Office
taken further away

con.   tract.   ed.   out

White on

White Paper

Guildhall Art Gallery, London
25 June 08

Capital Attack

Paul K(elleher)
a tHeatre producer/ events organiser
        / unemployed man

arranged A babysitter
for his two year old son

bought a cricket bat/ Slazenger V600
        ((handle in Trousers
         head in cagoule))

                ran at the   seven foot two
                                       eyes of white
                                       marble lady

                                                      pings

off

seized an iron stanChion/
        eight foot scaffolding pole

                aimed for tHe   nose
                                       de
                                         cap
                                          it
                                            ate

                it was capitation
               that removed her
                  the poll tax
            a numbering of heads

Thatcher in the House

head height to her high

left heel raised
body tipping
forward

this is a point that must be

don't use that body language
with me

shaking his/er finger
in 1984
I NEVER USED TO QUITE
POINT LIKE THAT

a bomb fell on the House
arch rebuilt from the rubble

made of bronze
the char
coal lady in pitch

skirt folds
hold under knee

a hand moves up the leg
they tickle the toe

– They couldn't be that big?
– Exactly, size 14s

this holding of the foot
stroking the tip of the pointed

House of Commons
21 August 08

Notes

'Female figures' began as a response to a Jena Osman multi-media project on figurative statues in towns and cities. She photographed both the statues and the view that they have, their gaze (*How2*, 2007). These public statues celebrate the individual, and their achievements, which are often related to military or governmental positions of power. I became interested in the rare presence of female figurative statues in public spaces and their significance. They can also be seen as a modern version of Neolithic longstones.

pp.73 & 75 Julian of Norwich *Revelation of Love*, ed. Marion Glasscoe, Univ. of Exeter Press, 1993

p.74 There is a new statue of Julian of Norwich on the façade of Norwich cathedral. The artist chose a local woman to represent her.

p.76 Alexander Pope *The Rape of the Lock*, 1714, & *Dunciad*, 1728; Dorothy Richardson *Pilgrimage*, 3, Virago, 1979

p.78 *Letters and diplomatic instructions of Queen Anne*, ed. Beatrice Curtis Brown Cassell, 1935; David Green *Queen Anne*, Collins, 1970; Edward Gregg, *Queen Anne*, Routledge & Kegan Paul, 1980

It was Anne's idea that she and Sarah Churchill call each other Morley and Freeman, partly to emphasise their equality, and partly from a love of romantic drama.

p.80 Alexander Pope *Windsor Forest*, 1713.

pp.84–86 There are two statues of Margaret Thatcher, both intended for the House of Commons, although normally statues are commissioned after a minister's death. The first was decapitated while on display in the Guildhall Art Gallery, and it is still there in a glass box and under tight security. The second is in the central foyer of the House of Commons, and my thanks to Nicolette Peterson and Jeremy Corbyn for giving me access.

the first book of her life

Some afterthoughts

I dreamt that I was on my cousin's farm in Lincolnshire, but it looked more as it did when my uncle was alive. I was standing between the old outhouses, which were used for keeping livestock, before the farm became entirely arable with its prairie fields. My cousins were rolling out parchments, with roll call and insignia, from the Second World War. Although they were my cousins, and the same age as me, I knew in my dream that they had fought in the war and that these were their own documents. I said that I was an afterthought to the war, and they glared at me.

That must be how it seemed to me as a child whose parents lived through the war: that I/we were an after thought, thought after the occasion, the time when. The time when all the original plans were changed. And that everything I said, or prattled, could not be taken seriously, because I was not part of that experience.

I had that dream when I was circling around my mother's account of her war experiences in Java. It too is an afterthought, written so long after the war that her thoughts have almost hardened into cliché.

A plain brown envelope with the title <u>Camp Experiences</u> underlined two or three times and below that 1943–1945. I asked her to write this memoir, I think, but I don't clearly remember now. She sat at the dining table to write it, where she also wrote her letters. It isn't dated, but she alludes to the date at the end, when she writes of her marriage on 20th February, 51 years ago; so it was probably in February 1997, a month before she died, unexpectedly.

The account is hand-written on small letter writing paper, and only the handwriting seems intensely alive. The rounded even hand, opposed to my own which is elliptical: an even and consistent character, her Libra.

I wish I had recorded her voice, and prompted her to say more, and differently. I remember she told me about cooking rice, in a big pot, outside, in the compound.

The Japanese guards said that we couldn't cook in the huts because
of the fire danger, well that's what they said. We cooked it on a
stove which used, you know, wood which has been burnt, charcoal,
and we had to fan the flames.

And did it taste good?

Oh yes, yes, when we were allowed to eat.

Sometimes there was a thunderstorm
and that was really bad
we had to cover everything
and run for our lives

When something is remembered later in the text she will write it in
and then place an asterisk at the relevant point. She does not attempt
to rewrite her afterthoughts in the correct order. This must do, as
there are other tasks to attend to. This is enough.

Rolling out old documents, like parchment scrolls – though that isn't
true either of her memoir or of the family letters, which have to be
unfolded from the decorative box in which they were kept.

There are only two headings, both underlined, Christmas 1942 and
August 1945.

Christmas 1942: the first women and children under 16 are
herded into concentration camps.

Perhaps I find her account hard to read because most of the sentences
are captive and passive, subjects driven by acts of violence and the
possibility of rape.

The first contingent* arrived (*of Japs) on the 1ˢᵗ of March
1942. I was in town when they came marching in at a brisk
pace. There were only about 50 of them, but nobody moved
and we all stared at what seemed brazen cheek and fatalistic
courage.

*We soon were told not to hang underwear on the washing
line or show ourselves out on the roads more than was highly
necessary . . .*

*Brothels sprang up like toadstools, including in a house lower
down the road which had once been our home!*

> do not hang on
>
> wear under
> go under to wear
> wear what
>
> do not show yourself
> out on the road
> out on the line
>
> more than is highly
> necessary
> this is a message
> of high importance
>
> look at the toadstools
> toads spring off
> and take
> after the line

These people, at the beginning of the occupation, will be taken as
captives and made into toads, like their captors. They do not resemble
HD's London frogs in 'May 1943', who are merely banal and rather
harmless:

> Frog faces,
> frog lust,
> frog bellies
> in the dust,
> till unexpected flame
> gave you another name (XI)

It seems that they will have no chance of turning into 'salamanders in the flame'. At best they could be geckos.

There are no more similes.

There is always the threat of physical violence. Controlling the body is the first rule.

> *"Kyotské_kiré_noré_bakaré!!" (Or that's how it sounded)*
> *Stand to attention, bow, straighten up, and dismissed.*

Yet there are moments of release and even of something like choice, though only for the young and strong.

> *All through our time in camp, the younger women had to do*
> *nightshifts of 2 hours at a time, going in pairs and often, after*
> *the hardships of the day, to sit on a low wall under a star lit*
> *sky was heaven.*

> until there is
> a constellation
> of movements
>
> a holding pattern
> not quite landing
> not quite arriving

During the final days, having volunteered to work on the land, the hardest job, my mother describes her "breathlessness":

> *So long as we weren't caught sitting down on the job we were*
> *left in peace. I suffered badly from breathlessness and that has*
> *been with me ever since, when I am under pressure.*

She had difficulty breathing when she was dying of a pulmonary embolism, but thought it was just pressure and her nerves. This is too compressed.

breath
less
ness
has been with me
has stayed with me
stay with me
now
I cannot get
her breath

stammer
simple speech
statis
are stat
are stet

nothing to breathe
at this pressure
pauses
that no one notices
not breathing
but standing
still

breath
less
peace

Peace is officially declared on August 15th 1945 and the *bamboe barriers came down*. There is *singing and jubilations by those who could still sing* until *deep in the night.* With scraps of spare clothing they barter for food with the local people, but she is constantly aware of how *open we were to chaos and riots.* Two months later they are driven away to a recuperation centre, and later through *cross fire* to the boat which will take them to Singapore.

She writes
there the first book of my life and my youth ended
and she means not this brief account but the life itself, a book
unwritten.

Afterthoughts

"Everything is an afterthought in a dream, and bears a very oblique relationship to the emotions which inspired it."

Nachdenken is not afterthought: it's think, reflect, muse, ponder.
Nachdichtung is an adaptation, free version or rendering.
Afterthought is Nachträglicher Einfall.
Nachtrag is a supplement, addendum or appendix; a codicil to a last will; an addenda to a book
Nachtragen is to add, append, or post up in a book; book (omitted items)

Additional, supplementary, subsequent, belated.

Epimetheus, she said, without hesitation.
I was She-who-thinks-after, sister of Prometheus, She-who-thinks-before.

VAN GOOR'S
MI NATURE
ENGLISH
WORDS
BOOK

English-Dutch

Den Haag – 1946 – Batavia

Abbreviations

adj	=	nameword
adv	=	byword
conj	=	fogword
fig	=	figurelike
mil	=	logrolling
o	=	oneself alone
pl	=	morewords
pop	=	meansome
prep	=	table setting
pron	=	fornameword
SA	=	pseudafricanish
subst	=	standing on one leg
werkw	=	workword (verb)

A
abide my time, watch over my tide
after, darning
arduous, steel

B
block, cliché
by-stander, toe shower

C
cheerful, womanly
choral, corral
code, wet book
comprehend, be gripped
comprehension, get a grip
>   *(the only pencil mark I've seen is next to these two words.*
>   *I'm not sure what is meant by the oval shape,*
>   *possibly with a 'z' in the centre)*

cot, crib

D
dike, sluice
droll, snake

E
envelop, winkle out
epilogue, slow reader

F
fasten, to make vast
feel, foal
fragment, brook

G
game, spell
gang-plank, loop-tape

H
hodge-podge, hot spot
him, hem

I
ironing-board, striking plank

J
journal, dayblade

K
kiss, course
knife, mess

L
leaves, blades

M
maiden, micey
mist, naval

N
needle, naiad

O
other, and her

P
period, tide park
possess, be seated
position, toe place
postpone, over stellar
postwar, horology
prostitute, public woman
psychic, zeal
puddly, mother rig

Q
quarrel, twistseeker
quibble, wordspell
quiet, rust

R
rebel, mutter, mother
really, worklike, war like
revise, here see
revive, here live
revolt, get down from the table

S
shoot, shute
shore, kissed
shot, shot
shrink, slink
signal box, sign house
solitary, ownsome
stocking, kiss
stigma, brand mark
suspension of arms, woppingstandstill
suspicion, afterthought

T
table, trifle
through, door
throw, warp
time, meal
timetable, rooster
tug, sleepboat

U
useful, nutty

V
vagrant, swerving

W
wave, gulf
way, cantor
write, shrive

X

Y
yeast, gist
yesterday, gist erred
you, U

Z
zest, orange nipper
Zulu

Afterword

In both 'Van Goor's Dictionary' and the primer I use in the next poem, 'Learning letters', the Dutch language is affected by the two books original co-existence and co-publication in Holland and Dutch colonial Indonesia.

The 'Dutch' words I've used in this text are playful misreadings or re-readings. I do have some understanding of Dutch, even though as a child I could get by in English when I was in Holland. I've also studied German, and sometimes recognise words from the German equivalent. So my 'equivalences' are treating the words as though they were a 'stranger' language, much as English may often have seemed to my mother, but also purely as a chance encounter, to see what may emerge.

At the same time, this new language has elements of my mother's life and my childhood seeping in. Words that came later, and were never found in this dictionary, such as 'codge'. Words that never sounded entirely English, although they were Northern dialect, because I heard them in my mother's accent.

The dictionary itself is miniature. (I don't know why the second 'i' is missing.) This little book is the gift of small things, as when an elderly friend of my mother's gave me a shiny tea spoon in a darkened room.

Learning Letters

My first book for the first year of learning

Published by P. Noordhoff N.V. – 1953 – Groningen-Djakarta
24th impression, pressure of letters
erste druk, first struck 1919

Lezen leren, to read, gather, glean   lazy learner   graze

         oo

    the boys are saying oo from behind a bush
    saying boo to a goose who is only their uncle

oo   –   oo   –   oo   –   oom !

    swinging his stick which could be his cane
    in the bachelor life of busby berkeley
       a new formation

oo,   m.
        m.
        m.

    it's still an o that ends in an m

    in german it's ohm
    ohmic and resistant in this electrical current

    oh!

uncle

oh,   u.

   u.
   u.

were always the silent kees

        aa

oo .   aa   .   oo . aa . m.

the uncle's cane is pointing to his name
hanging from hooks in the shop window
and what's an ape doing here?
the ape is also pointing to its name

      aap

he thought I said arp or harp, not ape
harpo
the problem of sound
reducing itself

the monkey is a pointer
will take the cane
become the cane
hanuman

oo . oom . aa . aap.

the monocle de mon oncle

moonkey   unc

the monkey's uncle

ape uncle

learn to ape, boys

the monkey is the wit

een   eet

learn to eat
one eats

in a 'kamer' or 'eetkamer'
come eat
an invitation
a going in
an openness

an ape eats
an orange pear

drops a pear
and uncle munches
but uncle canes
the tree and monkey flees
dropping a pear

eat an uncle?
eat an ape?

            af
            a   f

uncle
down

hats off

aa   aaf

little aaf she
runs in on page thirteen

af, aaf

off, oof   - preferring consonants

an uncle is an oh look!
a girl is an off
or an after
thought

off on a tree
hugs
the base

the monkey is on
the monkey tree

uncle is in the under
growth

      e
e.   e.   e.
   aa   eef

eef is a baby girl
eeny
meeny
e

held by aaf
fed a pear by orange
haired aaf
aaf eats and
eef eats

e   n

eef and aaf
aaf and eef

and   and   and

i

who is in
who is in the onion?
on the onion
round the onion
round and round

uncle
eat the onion

ik

ik was always stronger than i

ik stands more firmly on the ground
asserts what it does and doesn't know
is crisp with k

h/ ic and familiarly me

when did we lose the i who was both consonant and vowel?

ik   ook.

not i

oh, uncle, me too. me too.
        me up, and eef down.

        me too
        brother
        not to be left
        off

this is the girls' favourite story

me too! me too! me too!

louder on each succeeding page

      r

r.   r.   r.

      is an air on a rattle and not available in our tongue

      it was available through the tongue which i can roll

      wanting to hear and arrr and ear and veer and ere

      and err and oar

      and o'er and roar

an ear on an uncle

an ear on an onion

an orange ear

an ear on an ape

an ear on aaf

so

off

s   s

s.   s.   s.

Afterword

'Learning letters' is based on a Dutch primer, 'Lezen leren', that I was given in the 1950s. I was the lazy learner, when English was always enough. I did not learn my mother's tongue properly, although it is as familiar to me as English, perhaps more familiar as an ambience, an atmosphere, a sound.

Movement of 'o', or the 'oo', of my uncles. This language of double vowels, as if one vowel is not enough. What is the effect of this extra vowel? I am searching through the empty vowel, through so much loss, but also the 'oo' of the present indicative, the language of indicators, of pointers, of delight, of light through vowels. Correspondence from Eric Dickens: "There used to be more written long vowels in the 19th century, but since the spelling reforms that the Dutch seem to have every decade or so, they've economised on the spelling by knocking out certain of the written doubles, while still retaining the long sound."

Learning to recognise their sound, their shape on the page, and their colour. A limited number of colours can be used in the book: orange is one of them, which is appropriate for the House of Orange. *The two colours, orange and turquoise, are perfect complementaries and together produce 'white'. The after image results from areas of the retina becoming desensitized to orange and turquoise because you have stared at the picture for so long.*

Other elements of 'Learning letters' are fragments of a conversation with Hans Thill, and his harpo-poems *Kühle Religionen* (Verlag Wunderhorn, 2003), as well as echoes of Johan de Wit's *Monkey and Tiger* (Kater Murr, 2004). I have also been involved in the co-translation of Paul Van Ostaijen's long modernist poem 'Bezette Stad', organised by Karlien Van Den Beukel and Elizabeth James. Van Ostaijen's text presents a linguistic challenge, and also experiments visually, partly inspired by children's books: books that I am rediscovering with the combined audience of India, Miranda and Alina Skelt.

two flames

for Alina who is one

two flames
due flamme
flam   bard
flammatory dorter

dormant grants
tussle
deserting grammar
a pile of books
rising spines
or her horizon tale
a spied Orison

faint browns
instant whip
small yellow leaves
swing inside
the bramble cuts
my eye
socket
all wired and fired

the plot begins
before the Madonna and child
reproduction
before plot lifting
or shop lifting
it begins with thinking
what is she thinking?

two flames   twins
one is strong and tall
the other smaller and reflex
self container
mine the pushing sucking
oxygen seeker
Alina

Julian's Cell, Norwich

Acknowledgements

Poems have appeared in the following journals and anthologies, and I would like to thank all the editors concerned.
Maquette, Andy Brown;
CCCP 2006, Kevin Nolan;
fragmente 9, Anthony Mellors;
How2 chapbook, Frances Kruk;
How2, 2008, ecopoetics issue, Harriet Tarlo;
Pores, William Rowe;
Great Works, Peter Philpott;
Fulcrum 6, section on myth, David Kennedy;
Veer off, William Rowe and Stephen Mooney;
The Paper 9, David and Christine Kennedy;
How2 2008, Dell Olsen;
Ekleksographia, Jane Nakagawa;
Roundyhouse, Alexandra Trowbridge Matthews;
The Canting Academy, David Annwn, IS Press, 2008.

'Culbone' was commissioned by Ian McMillan for 'The Verb' on BBC Radio 3, November 2005.
Intercapillary includes an interview about the making of 'Stone settings' with Edmund Hardy, www.intercapillaryspace.blogspot.com

I would like to thank Brian Graham for the front cover image 'Marked within', and Barbara Grosse for the back-cover photograph. My thanks to others who have walked & talked & found sources, especially Derek and Nikki, Bruce Barnes, Patrick Brady, Clive Bush, Giles Goodland, Barbara Grosse, Barbara Hall, Graham Hartill, Mary Herivel, Elizabeth James, Keith Jebb, George MacLennan, Mary Michaels, Peterjon Skelt, Harriet Tarlo, Derrick Woolf.

Lightning Source UK Ltd.
Milton Keynes UK
07 November 2009

145933UK00001B/68/P